# Darting
# Dragonflies

by Robin Nelson

first step nonfiction

Lerner Publications ◆ Minneapolis

**LERNER**

**SOURCE**

Expand learning beyond the printed book. Download free, complementary educational resources for this book from our website, www.lernerresource.com.

The images in this book are used with the permission of: © iStockphoto.com/RoseMaryBush, p. 4; © John Kirwin Photography/Moment Open/Getty Images, p. 5; © ZUMA Press, Inc./Alamy, p. 6; © Paul Reeves/Dreamstime.com, p. 7; © iStockphoto.com/abzerit, p. 8; © Dwight Kuhn, p. 9; © Rolf Nussbaumer Photography/Alamy, pp. 10, 13; © Phil Degginger/Animals Animals, p. 11; © Michael Durham/Minden Pictures/Newscom, pp. 12, 20; © David Lester/Alamy, p. 14; © Donna Brunet/Animals Animals, p. 15; © Rkhalil/Dreamstime.com, p. 16; © Brian P. Kenney/Animals Animals, p. 17; © Toni Ard/Moment Open/Getty Images, p. 18; © Mark Chappell/Animals Animals, p. 19; © iStockphoto.com/Christopher Futcher, p. 21; © Abeselom Zerit/Dreamstime.com, p. 22. Front cover: © iStockphoto.com/abzerit.

Main body text set in ITC Avant Garde Gothic Std Medium 21/25. Typeface provided by International Typeface Corp.

Lerner Publications Company
A division of Lerner Publishing Group, Inc.
241 First Avenue North
Minneapolis, MN 55401 USA

For reading levels and more information, look up this title at www.lernerbooks.com.

Library of Congress Cataloging-in-Publication Data

Names: Nelson, Robin, 1971– author.
Title: Darting dragonflies / by Robin Nelson.
Description: Minneapolis : Lerner Publications, [2016] | Series: First step nonfiction. Backyard critters | Audience: Ages 5–8. | Audience: K to grade 3. | Includes index.
Identifiers: LCCN 2015041872 | ISBN 9781512408836 (lb : alk. paper) | ISBN 9781512412208 (pb : alk. paper) | ISBN 9781512410013 (eb pdf)
Subjects: LCSH: Dragonflies—Juvenile literature.
Classification: LCC QL520 .N4487 2016 | DDC 595.7/33—dc23     6908566
LC record available at http://lccn.loc.gov/2015041872

Manufactured in the United States of America
1 – CG – 7/15/16

# Table of Contents

# Dragonfly Bodies

Dragonflies are **insects** with long bodies.

Blue and green are common colors for dragonflies.

They can be many different colors.

Dragonflies have two sets of large wings.

Dragonfly wings look thin, but these insects are strong fliers.

You can see through their wings.

Dragonflies have huge eyes.

Dragonflies can see insects flying in front of them or behind them.

They use their eyes to look for **prey**.

Dragonflies have six legs.

They use their long legs to catch prey.

# Where to Find Dragonflies

Dragonflies come out when it is warm and sunny.

They live near lakes,
streams, and ponds.

This dragonfly lays her eggs in the water.

Dragonfly eggs can be found in water or on plants near water.

Young dragonflies are called nymphs.

Young dragonflies live in the water before becoming adults.

# Food

Dragonflies **hunt** for food as they fly.

They eat other insects.

# What Dragonflies Do

Dragonflies fly faster than most insects.

They can quickly change directions.

Dragonflies can even **hover** in one place.

But they are very hard to catch!

# Dragonfly Parts

wings

body

eyes

legs

# Glossary

**hover** – to float in the air without moving

**hunt** – to chase and kill for food

**insects** – small animals with six legs.  Insects also often have wings.

**prey** – an animal or insect that is killed for food

# Index